Oink and Gobble
and the
'No One Can Ever Know Secret'

This Book Belongs to:

_____

Imagination

"Laughter is timeless,
imagination has no age,
and dreams are forever."
Walt Disney

"For with God, nothing is impossible."
Luke 1:37

"Everything you can imagine is real."
Pablo Picasso

Oink and Gobble
and the
'No One Can Ever Know Secret'

by
Norman Whaler

Illustrated by
Mohammad Shayan

Edited by
Ellie Firestone

Beneath Another Sky Books

In a farm town called Little Bottom, there lived a farmer and his wife with their two children, whom all the animals on the farm just called Girl and Boy. The farmer raised turkeys, chickens, cows, pigs, and even had a dog. It was just like animal kingdom on the farm!

On one side of the farm was the farmhouse where the farmer lived with his family. But this story is not about the farmer or his wife. This story is about the animals on the farm. There was Oink the pig, Gobble the turkey, Moo the cow, and many others.

All the animals on the farm had a BIG secret and they had all sworn to protect that secret from all the humans.

'The No One Can Ever Know Secret!'

"We must never let them know! Never-ever!"
Gobble had said to Oink many, many times.
"Not farmerman, farmerwoman, or Girl or Boy."

"Hey Gobble! Do I have a big nose?"
Oink asked, not paying much attention to
Gobble because he was looking at
himself in a puddle of water.

"No, of course not! You just have a small face!"
Gobble said, laughing at how easily
distracted Oink could be at times.

Oink was a curious young pig with a red
nose, a curly tail, and short, fat legs.
He wanted to learn everything
about the world he lived in. He
especially liked to listen to the
farmer's children talking, and he had heard all
about aliens, and bigfoot, and so many other
mysterious things! He often wondered
when the aliens would come and
visit with their big spaceship.

Oink and Gobble were best friends, but they couldn't have been more different. And to see them together was certainly a strange sight! They were like the North and South Poles, yet they never fought. Where Oink was adventurous and curious about everything, Gobble was cautious and calm and practical.

Now, most of the other animals thought Oink was crazy because of his alien or bigfoot stories, but Gobble always enjoyed hearing about Oink's fantastic ideas.

"I think that Oink may be a few sandwiches short of a picnic," Bark the dog would often say, and all the other animals would shake their heads in sad agreement.

Today, Oink seemed unusually excited. This made Gobble smile as she always looked forward to hearing Oink's latest crazy idea.

"Oink! Oink!" Oink made his pig sound.

"What?" Gobble asked, pouting her beak.

"Oink, oink, squeal!" Oink said.

"Whaaaaat?"
again questioned Gobble.

"Shhhhhhhhh! We're not supposed to let the humans know we can talk!"

"Well, I think your pig noises are working," laughed Gobble.
"I certainly didn't understand you!"

"No! Be serious! I have to tell you something!" Oink whispered, excitedly running in circles around Gobble.

"OK! OK! No problem!" Gobble said,
now laughing even more at her best friend who
had begun dancing around her.
"So, why are we whispering again?" Gobble asked.
She was expecting another bigfoot story
and was happy to play along.

Oink looked to his right and then to his left,
checking to see if anyone could overhear them.
"I think they're on to us!"
Oink whispered.

Gobble looked to her right and then to her left,
teasing Oink. "WHO's on to WHO?"

Oink just couldn't contain himself any longer. The words exploded out of his mouth.

"The Humans...

They may know we can

TALK!"

"What?

What do you mean? Why would you say that?"
Gobble asked, her eyes wide.
She now feared the worst.

"Well..." Oink began, looking down and trying
his best not to look too guilty.
"Possibly... maybe... I'm not sure... but she may
have... uhm... overheard me."

Gobble's eyes grew even wider.
"You know the rules!
No human can ever know the

'No One Can
Ever Know Secret!'"

whispered a now quite frightened Gobble. "It could
change everything! They're just
not ready to know!"

"I know! I know! I know!" said Oink in a frantic voice. "It's not like I wanted her to know!"

"Wait... What??

Who's 'her'?" Gobble asked, wondering now what really was going on with Oink.

"Girl!" Oink exclaimed. "Girl is always watching me!"

"She is?" questioned Gobble, now thinking this was just Oink's imagination again.

"Yes!" replied Oink. "If I'm eating, she's there. If I'm having fun in the mud, she's there. If I'm going to the... well, you know... she's there! I mean, really! Can I have some privacy, please? She must know we can talk! Why else would she be following me around?"

Oink knew this was serious and he nervously smiled and tried to be brave in front of Gobble. How could he explain this to all the other animals?

"Well, we don't know anything for sure," said Gobble, but Oink continued on with his story as if he hadn't heard Gobble.

"And if I'm talking to you, she's..." Oink stopped in mid-sentence as he saw Girl standing in the yard and starring right at him! Not knowing what else to do, Oink did the first thing that came to his mind. He screamed in panic and ran!

"Run!
Run for your life!"

Gobble didn't know why Oink was screaming or running, but she decided the best thing to do was just run like Oink and ask later!

"Gobble, gobble, gobble, gobble," Gobble squawked in fright as she ran as fast as she could.

Through the barn and into the house, out the backdoor and over the dog, into the pasture and out again, past the chickens and around the pond, Oink and Gobble ran and ran. The dog was barking, the goat was jumping, and the chickens went flying into the air. All the animals were in an uproar with all this excitement!

But always, there was Girl right on their heels. They just couldn't shake her off!

"Wow! This has got to be the worst escape ever!" yelled Gobble as they both continued to run away from Girl who was never very far behind them.

"Gobble, wait... wait... I think we lost her," Oink gasped. They stopped to rest, huffing and puffing. It had been a long time since Oink had to run anywhere. And why should he? He definitely didn't want to be skinny like Gobble. He loved being fat!

But when they turned around... there was Girl standing next to the farmer.

"Oh, no…"

Oink just gave up. There was nothing he could do. The secret was out and it was the end of all the farm animals. Despite his best effort, the end of the world had come.

Girl just stood there... looking right at him.
Not at Gobble, or Bark, or Moo, or Quack,
but only at him!

"Him, Daddy! I want him!" Girl screamed in
delight, jumping up and down.

"SQUEAL?"

Oink exclaimed
(which meant "WHAT?" in pig language).

"OK, Princess," said the farmerman.
"He's all yours!"

"My very own pet!" she said.
"I'll always love you!"

HUH?

It now seemed to Oink that maybe the
situation wasn't what he had thought it was.
Maybe, just maybe, the
'No One Can Ever Know Secret'
was STILL a secret!

Could it be true?
Could he be that lucky?

YES!

The secret WAS safe, he now realized.

"Whewwww, that was way too close,"
he thought to himself.

And he also thought that maybe he could get
used to all these wonderful, wonderful hugs!

Oink and Gobble
and the
'No One Can Ever Know Secret'

Beneath Another Sky Books

Copyright © 2018 by Norman Whaler
All rights reserved. No part of this book may be used or reproduced by any means, graphic, electronic, or mechanical, including photocopying, recording, taping or by any information storage retrieval system without the written permission of the publisher, except in the case of brief quotations embodied in critical articles and reviews.

Book design copyright © 2018 Norman Whaler
Cover art and Illustrations by Mohammad Shayan
Interior book design by Norman Whaler
Edited by Ellie Firestone

Oink and Gobble Series Book 1

Library of Congress Catalogue Number: 2018900271
ISBN Hardcover 9781948131209
ISBN Epub 9781948131216
ISBN Kindle 9781948131223

Also Available in Spanish

normanwhaler.com
fiverr.com/shayan777

Printed in the USA

normanwhaler.com

Other Books by Norman Whaler

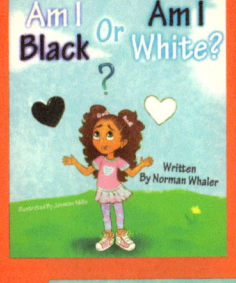
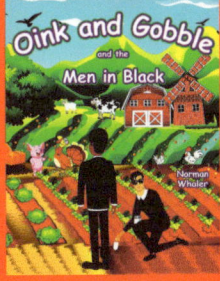

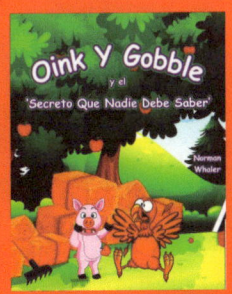
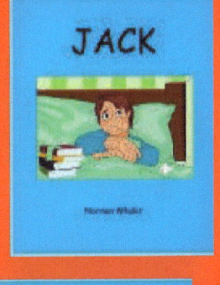
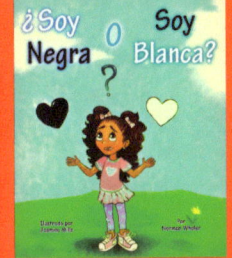
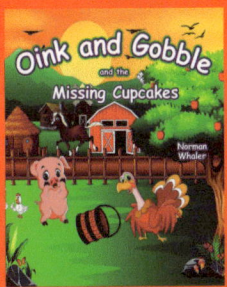
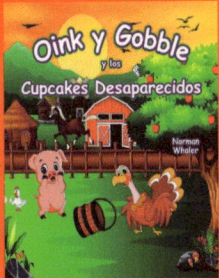
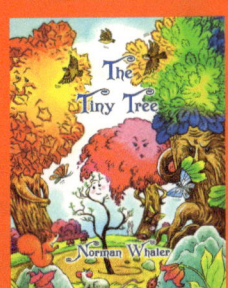
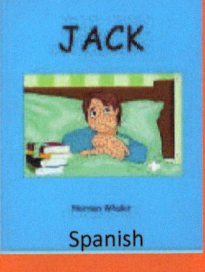

Spanish

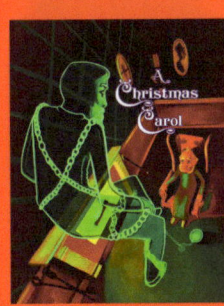
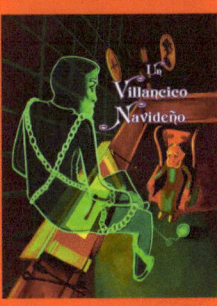
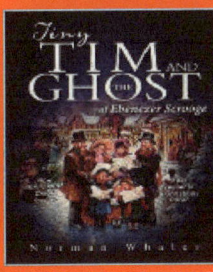
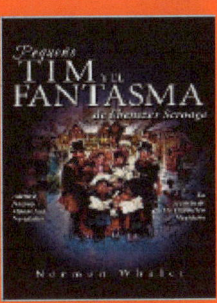
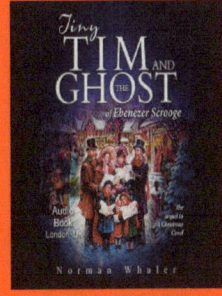

Audio Book Mp3

Jokes

Why was 6 scared of 7? Because 7 8 9.

Why does a seagull fly over the sea?
Because if it flew over a bay, it would be a baygull.

What kind of tree fits in your hand?
A palm tree.

Where would you find an elephant?
The same place you lost her.

What was the name of the wife of George Washington?
Mrs. Washington.

How do you get a squirrel to like you?
Act like a nut.

What did the banana say to the dog?
Nothing. Bananas can't talk.

What time is it when a clock strikes 13?
Time to get a new clock.

Why shouldn't you write with a broken pencil?
Because it's pointless.

Are you a good detective? How many animals are on page 1 of the story? (The answer is on the cow bell on page 5 of the story).

www.ingramcontent.com/pod-product-compliance
Lightning Source LLC
Chambersburg PA
CBHW041503220426
43661CB00016B/1244